100 Greatest *Love* Poems

100 Greatest Love Poems

Published by
Rupa Publications India Pvt. Ltd 2021
7/16, Ansari Road, Daryaganj
New Delhi 110002

Sales centres:
Allahabad Bengaluru Chennai
Hyderabad Jaipur Kathmandu
Kolkata Mumbai

Copyright © Rupa Publications India Pvt. Ltd 2021

All rights reserved.

No part of this publication may be reproduced, transmitted, or stored in a retrieval system, in any form or by any means, electronic, mechanical, photocopying, recording or otherwise, without the prior permission of the publisher.

ISBN: 978-93-90918-07-2

First impression 2021

10 9 8 7 6 5 4 3 2 1

The moral right of the author has been asserted.

Printed at Thomson Press India Ltd, Faridabad

This book is sold subject to the condition that it shall not, by way of trade or otherwise, be lent, resold, hired out, or otherwise circulated, without the publisher's prior consent, in any form of binding or cover other than that in which it is published.

Contents

A Note		*xiii*
1.	1 Corinthians 13:4–7	1
	The World English Bible	
2.	A Poem by Mir Taqi Mir	2
	Translated by Edward Powys Mathers	
3.	On Love	3
	Kahlil Gibran	
4.	Ode to Anactoria	6
	Sappho, Translated by John Myers O'Hara	
5.	How Do I Love Thee? (Sonnet 43)	8
	Elizabeth Barrett Browning	
6.	Shall I Compare Thee to a Summer's Day? (Sonnet 18)	9
	William Shakespeare	
7.	Ode to Psyche	10
	John Keats	
8.	A Red, Red Rose	13
	Robert Burns	
9.	She Walks in Beauty	14
	George Gordon Noel, Lord Byron	
10.	The Songs of Kabir XI	15
	Translated by Rabindranath Tagore	
11.	Song of Syria	19
	Translated by Edward Powys Mathers	
12.	I Am Not Yours	20
	Sara Teasdale	
13.	The Face of Helen	21
	Christopher Marlowe	

14.	Amoretti LXXV: One Day I Wrote her Name *Edmund Spenser*	22
15.	Her Lips Are Copper Wire *Jean Toomer*	23
16.	To His Coy Mistress *Andrew Marvell*	24
17.	What Lips My Lips Have Kissed, and Where, and Why (Sonnet XLIII) *Edna St. Vincent Millay*	26
18.	This is Love: A Selection from the Divani Shamsi Tabriz *Jalalu'd-din Rumi, Translated by Frederick Hadland Davis*	27
19.	I Shall Forget You Presently, My Dear (Sonnet IV) *Edna St. Vincent Millay*	28
20.	Never Give All the Heart *W. B. Yeats*	29
21.	I Do Not Love Thee *Caroline Elizabeth Sarah Norton*	33
22.	Love's Secret *William Blake*	34
23.	Now *Robert Browning*	35
24.	Let Me Not to the Marriage of True Minds (Sonnet 116) *William Shakespeare*	36
25.	To My Dear and Loving Husband *Anne Bradstreet*	37
26.	Love *Samuel Taylor Coleridge*	38
27.	The Good-Morrow *John Donne*	42

28.	Invitation to Love *Paul Laurence Dunbar*	43
29.	An Indian Love Song *Sarojini Naidu*	44
30.	Give All to Love *Ralph Waldo Emerson*	46
31.	Love's Marvellous Ways *Akka Mahadevi*	51
32.	Of Love: A Sonnet *Robert Herrick*	52
33.	Paradise Lost, Book IV, Lines 639–652 *John Milton*	53
34.	A Ditty *Sir Philip Sidney*	54
35.	We Two, How Long We Were Fool'd *Walt Whitman*	55
36.	The Awakening *James Weldon Johnson*	57
37.	Vivien's Song *Alfred, Lord Tennyson*	58
38.	The Definition of Love *Andrew Marvell*	59
39.	Amores (I) *E. E. Cummings*	61
40.	Amores (II) *E.E. Cummings*	63
41.	When You Are Old *W. B. Yeats*	67
42.	The Sea of Glass *Ezra Pound*	68

43.	Her Voice *Oscar Wilde*	69
44.	All Love Letters Are Ridiculous *Fernando Pessoa*	71
45.	Morning at the Window *T. S. Eliot*	73
46.	The Sun Rising *John Donne*	74
47.	Take All My Loves, My Love, Yea, Take Them All (Sonnet 40) *William Shakespeare*	76
48.	Since Brass, Nor Stone, Nor Earth, Nor Boundless Sea (Sonnet 65) *William Shakespeare*	77
49.	Song: to Celia ['Drink to Me Only with Thine Eyes'] *Ben Jonson*	78
50.	I Love You *Ella Wheeler Wilcox*	79
51.	Monna Innominata [Loved You First] *Christina Rossetti*	83
52.	Sylvia *George Etherege*	84
53.	Endymion *Henry Wadsworth Longfellow*	85
54.	Coldness in Love *D. H. Lawrence*	87
55.	Love *Rupert Brooke*	89
56.	Meeting at Night *Robert Browning*	90

57.	Take, Oh, Take Those Lips Away *John Fletcher*	91
58.	Remembrance *Emily Brontë*	92
59.	Wild Nights — Wild Nights! *Emily Dickinson*	94
60.	The Passionate Shepherd to His Love *Christopher Marlowe*	95
61.	Camomile Tea *Katherine Mansfield*	99
62.	If Thou Must Love Me (Sonnet 14) *Elizabeth Barrett Browning*	101
63.	Unending Love *Rabindranath Tagore*	102
64.	Love Song *Rainer Maria Rilke, Translated by Jessie Lamont*	104
65.	Sometimes with One I Love *Walt Whitman*	105
66.	To O. E. A. *Claude McKay*	106
67.	Evening Song *Willa Cather*	108
68.	Sonnet XLIV [For Thee the Sun Doth Daily Rise, and Set] *George Santayana*	109
69.	Why I Love Thee? *Sadakichi Hartmann*	110
70.	Oh, Oh, You Will Be Sorry for that Word! *Edna St. Vincent Millay*	111
71.	The Difference *Thomas Hardy*	115

72.	Love and a Question *Robert Frost*	**116**
73.	The Clod and the Pebble *William Blake*	**118**
74.	Because She Would Ask Me Why I Loved Her *Christopher Brennan*	**119**
75.	Annabel Lee *Edgar Allen Poe*	**120**
76.	To the Fair Clorinda *Aphra Behn*	**122**
77.	Jenny Kiss'd Me *Leigh Hunt*	**124**
78.	A Winter's Tale *D. H. Lawrence*	**125**
79.	The Nymph's Reply to the Shepherd *Sir Walter Raleigh*	**126**
80.	Air and Angels *John Donne*	**128**
81.	Epitaph *Lady Katherine Dyer*	**133**
82.	From The Princess: Now Sleeps the Crimson Petal *Alfred, Lord Tennyson*	**134**
83.	Donal Og *Isabella Augusta, Lady Gregory*	**135**
84.	Whoso List to Hunt, I Know Where Is an Hind *Thomas Wyatt*	**137**
85.	They Flee from Me *Thomas Wyatt*	**138**
86.	At Last *Elizabeth Akers Allen*	**139**

87.	Perfect Woman *William Wordsworth*	141
88.	Aedh Wishes for the Cloths of Heaven *W. B. Yeats*	143
89.	Love and Friendship *Emily Brontë*	144
90.	The Mortal Lease *Edith Wharton*	145
91.	A Triad *Christina Rossetti*	149
92.	I am Mad with Love *Mirabai*	150
93.	Song *Paul Laurence Dunbar*	151
94.	The Sorrow of True Love *Edward Thomas*	152
95.	XXIII [Places among the Stars] *Stephen Crane*	153
96.	Hid My Love *John Clare*	154
97.	The City is Peopled *H. D.*	156
98.	To Helen *Edgar Allan Poe*	157
99.	When I Heard at the Close of Day *Walt Whitman*	158
100.	The Lovers *Jalalu'd-din Rumi, Translated by Shahram Shiva*	160

A Note

In the 1960s, Aram Saroyan's one-word poem left everyone puzzled—how could a misspelled word be considered poetry?

The poem,

>   lighght

If you consider 'lighght' as a poem, you might be scratching your head too but look at it as a photograph, and perhaps it can be understood better. Lighght is something you see rather than read. 'The difference between 'lighght' and another type of poem with more words is that it doesn't have a reading process,' says Saroyan.

Now, we come to the most important question of all. What is a poem really?

To my mind, a poem is a home for our deeply felt emotions, a secret hiding place. A poem is what reminds us of the playfulness of language, of the ability to put into words the unnameable emotions—sadness, rage, humour, wit and of course, the most favourite of all—love.

This book is an attempt at curating some of the most well-written and well-loved poems of the world. However, curating such a list is no mean feat. Be it the subjectivity of what should or shouldn't be considered 'greatest' as well as copyright issues has led to the non-inclusion of many poems that we love and have found in them, comfort and solace. Therefore, this book doesn't claim to be the last word on love poems. Instead, it is an effort at inclusivity, to provide a home for classic, lesser known, devotional as well as queer love poems, to provide a secret hiding place for feelings of love, of heartache, of disappointment, of sheer joy.

1

1 Corinthians 13:4–7

The World English Bible

Love is patient and is kind;love doesn't envy. Love doesn't brag, is not proud, doesn't behave itself inappropriately, doesn't seek its own way, is not provoked, takes no account of evil; doesn't rejoice in unrighteousness, but rejoices with the truth; bears all things, believes all things, hopes all things, endures all things.

2

A Poem by Mir Taqi Mir

Translated by Edward Powys Mathers

Love brings tiny sweat into your hair
Like stars marching in the dead of the night.
Joy fills my eyes, remembering your hair, with tears,
   And these tears roll and shine;
Into my thoughts is woven a dark night with raindrops
   And the rolling and shining of love songs.

3

On Love

Kahlil Gibran

Then said Almitra, Speak to us of Love.
And he raised his head and looked upon the people,
and there fell a stillness upon them.
And with a great voice he said:
When love beckons to you, follow him,
Though his ways are hard and steep.
And when his wings enfold you yield to him,
Though the sword hidden among his pinions may wound you.
And when he speaks to you believe in him,
Though his voice may shatter your dreams
as the north wind lays waste the garden.

For even as love crowns you so shall he crucify you.
Even as he is for your growth so is he for your pruning.
Even as he ascends to your height and caresses
your tenderest branches that quiver in the sun,
So shall he descend to your roots and shake them
in their clinging to the earth.

Like sheaves of corn he gathers you unto himself
He threshes you to make your naked.
He sifts you to free you from your husks.

He grinds you to whiteness.
He kneads you until you are pliant;
And then he assigns you to his sacred fire,
that you may become sacred bread for God's sacred feast.

All these things shall love do unto you that you
may know the secrets of your heart, and in that
knowledge become a fragment of Life's heart.
But if in your heart you would seek only
love's peace and love's pleasure,
Then it is better for you that you cover your nakedness
and pass out of love's threshing-floor,
Into the seasonless world where you shall laugh,
But not all of your laughter, and weep,
but not all of your tears.

Love gives naught but itself and takes naught but from itself.
Love possesses not nor would it be possessed;
For love is sufficient unto love.

When you love you should not say, 'God is in my heart,'
but rather, 'I am in the heart of God.'
And think not you can direct the course of love, for love,
if it finds you worthy, directs your course.

Love has no other desire but to fulfil itself.
But if you love and must needs have
desires, let these be your desires:
To melt and be like a running brook that

sings its melody to the night.
To know the pain of too much tenderness.
To be wounded by your own understanding of love;
And to bleed willingly and joyfully.
To wake at dawn with a winged heart and
give thanks for another day of loving;
To rest at the noon hour and meditate love's ecstasy;
To return home at eventide with gratitude;
And then to sleep with a prayer for the beloved in your heart
and a song of praise upon your lips.

4

Ode to Anactoria

Sappho, Translated by John Myers O'Hara

Peer of Gods to me is the man thy presence
Crowns with joy; who hears, as he sits beside thee,
Accents sweet of thy lips the silence breaking,
With lovely laughter;

Tones that make the heart in my bosom flutter,
For if I, the space of a moment even,
Near to thee come, any word I would utter
Instantly fails me;

Vain my stricken tongue would a whisper fashion,
Subtly under my skin runs fire ecstatic;
Straightway mists surge dim to my eyes and leave them
Reft of their vision;

Echoes ring in my ears; a trembling seizes
All my body bathed in soft perspiration;
Pale as grass I grow in my passion's madness,
Like one insensate;

But must I dare all, since to me unworthy,
Bliss thy beauty brings that a God might envy;
Never yet was fervid woman a fairer
Image of Kypris.

Ah! undying Daughter of God, befriend me!
Calm my blood that thrills with impending transport;
Feed my lips the murmur of words to stir her
Bosom to pity;

Overcome with kisses her faintest protest,
Melt her mood to mine with amorous touches,
Till her low assent and her sigh's abandon
Lure me to rapture.

How Do I Love Thee? (Sonnet 43)

Elizabeth Barrett Browning

How do I love thee? Let me count the ways.
I love thee to the depth and breadth and height
My soul can reach, when feeling out of sight
For the ends of being and ideal grace.
I love thee to the level of every day's
Most quiet need, by sun and candle-light.
I love thee freely, as men strive for right.
I love thee purely, as they turn from praise.
I love thee with the passion put to use
In my old griefs, and with my childhood's faith.
I love thee with a love I seemed to lose
With my lost saints. I love thee with the breath,
Smiles, tears, of all my life; and, if God choose,
I shall but love thee better after death.

Shall I Compare Thee to a Summer's Day? (Sonnet 18)

William Shakespeare

Shall I compare thee to a summer's day?
Thou art more lovely and more temperate.
Rough winds do shake the darling buds of May,
And summer's lease hath all too short a date.
Sometime too hot the eye of heaven shines,
And often is his gold complexion dimmed;
And every fair from fair sometime declines,
By chance, or nature's changing course, untrimmed;
But thy eternal summer shall not fade,
Nor lose possession of that fair thou ow'st,
Nor shall death brag thou wand'rest in his shade,
When in eternal lines to Time thou grow'st.
    So long as men can breathe, or eyes can see,
    So long lives this, and this gives life to thee.

7

Ode to Psyche

John Keats

O Goddess! hear these tuneless numbers, wrung
      By sweet enforcement and remembrance dear,
And pardon that thy secrets should be sung
      Even into thine own soft-conched ear:
Surely I dreamt to-day, or did I see
      The winged Psyche with awaken'd eyes?
I wander'd in a forest thoughtlessly,
      And, on the sudden, fainting with surprise,
Saw two fair creatures, couched side by side
      In deepest grass, beneath the whisp'ring roof
      Of leaves and trembled blossoms, where there ran
      A brooklet, scarce espied:
Mid hush'd, cool-rooted flowers, fragrant-eyed,
      Blue, silver-white, and budded Tyrian,
They lay calm-breathing, on the bedded grass;
      Their arms embraced, and their pinions too;
      Their lips touch'd not, but had not bade adieu,
As if disjoined by soft-handed slumber,
And ready still past kisses to outnumber
      At tender eye-dawn of aurorean love:
      The winged boy I knew;
But who wast thou, O happy, happy dove?

          His Psyche true!
O latest born and loveliest vision far
        Of all Olympus' faded hierarchy!
Fairer than Phoebe's sapphire-region'd star,
        Or Vesper, amorous glow-worm of the sky;
Fairer than these, though temple thou hast none,
          Nor altar heap'd with flowers;
Nor virgin-choir to make delicious moan
          Upon the midnight hours;
No voice, no lute, no pipe, no incense sweet
        From chain-swung censer teeming;
No shrine, no grove, no oracle, no heat
        Of pale-mouth'd prophet dreaming.
O brightest! though too late for antique vows,
        Too, too late for the fond believing lyre,
When holy were the haunted forest boughs,
        Holy the air, the water, and the fire;
Yet even in these days so far retir'd
        From happy pieties, thy lucent fans,
        Fluttering among the faint Olympians,
I see, and sing, by my own eyes inspir'd.
So let me be thy choir, and make a moan
          Upon the midnight hours;
Thy voice, thy lute, thy pipe, thy incense sweet
        From swinged censer teeming;
Thy shrine, thy grove, thy oracle, thy heat
        Of pale-mouth'd prophet dreaming.
Yes, I will be thy priest, and build a fane
        In some untrodden region of my mind,

Where branched thoughts, new grown with pleasant pain,
      Instead of pines shall murmur in the wind:
Far, far around shall those dark-cluster'd trees
      Fledge the wild-ridged mountains steep by steep;
And there by zephyrs, streams, and birds, and bees,
      The moss-lain Dryads shall be lull'd to sleep;
And in the midst of this wide quietness
A rosy sanctuary will I dress
With the wreath'd trellis of a working brain,
      With buds, and bells, and stars without a name,
With all the gardener Fancy e'er could feign,
      Who breeding flowers, will never breed the same:
And there shall be for thee all soft delight
      That shadowy thought can win,
A bright torch, and a casement ope at night,
      To let the warm Love in!

8

A Red, Red Rose

Robert Burns

O my luve's like a red, red rose,
That's newly sprung in June;
O my luve's like the melodie
That's sweetly played in tune.
As fair art thou, my bonnie lass,
So deep in luve am I;
And I will luve thee still, my dear,
Till a' the seas gang dry.
Till a' the seas gang dry, my dear,
And the rocks melt wi' the sun:
O I will love thee still, my dear,
While the sands o' life shall run.
And fare thee weel, my only luve,
And fare thee weel awhile!
And I will come again, my luve,
Though it were ten thousand mile.

She Walks in Beauty

George Gordon Noel, Lord Byron

I.
She walks in beauty, like the night
Of cloudless climes and starry skies;
And all that's best of dark and bright
Meet in her aspect and her eyes:
Thus mellowed to that tender light
Which heaven to gaudy day denies.

II.
One shade the more, one ray the less,
Had half impaired the nameless grace
Which waves in every raven tress,
Or softly lightens o'er her face;
Where thoughts serenely sweet express
How pure, how dear their dwelling place.

III.
And on that cheek, and o'er that brow,
So soft, so calm, yet eloquent,
The smiles that win, the tints that glow,
But tell of days in goodness spent,
A mind at peace with all below,
A heart whose love is innocent!

10

The Songs of Kabir XI

Translated by Rabindranath Tagore

I. 131. *nis' din khelat rahî sakhiyân sang*
I played day and night with my comrades,
and now I am greatly afraid.
So high is my Lord's palace, my heart trembles to mount
its stairs: yet I must not be shy, if I would enjoy His love.
My heart must cleave to my Lover; I must withdraw
my veil, and meet Him with all my body:
Mine eyes must perform the ceremony of the lamps of love.
Kabîr says: 'Listen to me, friend: he understands who loves.
If you feel not love's longing for your Beloved One, it is vain
to adorn your body, vain to put unguent on your eyelids.'

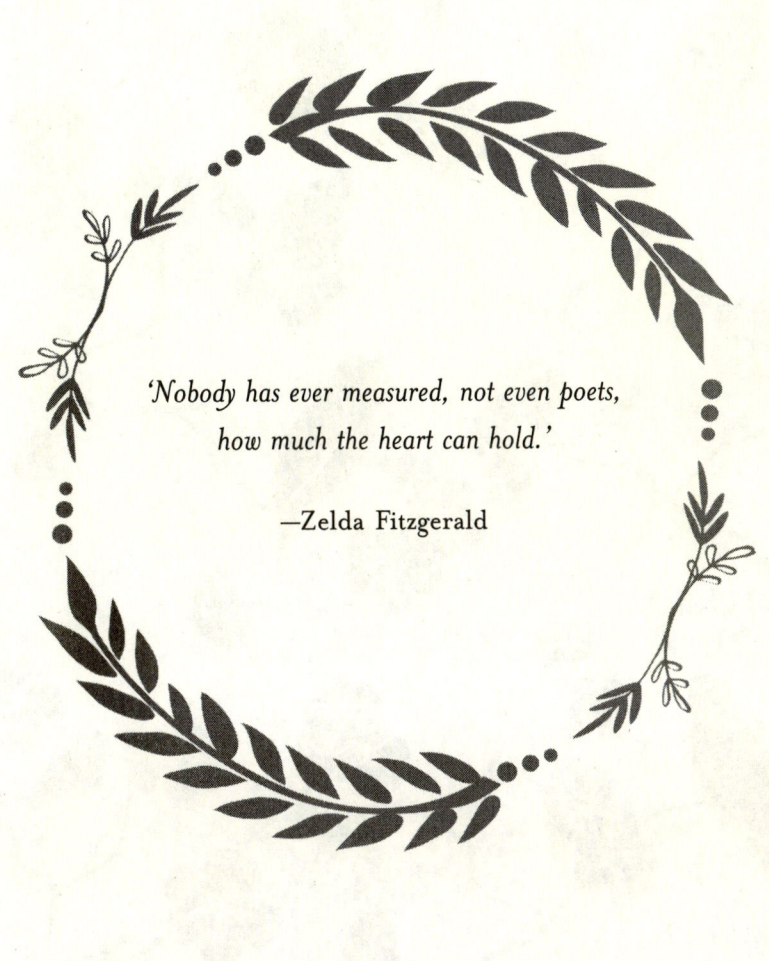

'Nobody has ever measured, not even poets, how much the heart can hold.'

—Zelda Fitzgerald

Song of Syria

Translated by Edward Powys Mathers

Kill me if you will not love me.
   Here are flints;
Ram down the heavy bullet, little leopard,
   On the black powder.

Only you must not shoot me through the head,
   Nor touch my heart;
Because my head is full of the ways of you
   And my heart is dead.

12

I Am Not Yours

Sara Teasdale

I am not yours, not lost in you,
Not lost, although I long to be
Lost as a candle lit at noon,
Lost as a snowflake in the sea.
You love me, and I find you still
A spirit beautiful and bright,
Yet I am I, who long to be
Lost as a light is lost in light.
Oh plunge me deep in love—put out
My senses, leave me deaf and blind,
Swept by the tempest of your love,
A taper in a rushing wind.

The Face of Helen

Christopher Marlowe

Was this the face that launch'd a thousand ships,
And burnt the topless towers of Ilium?
Sweet Helen, make me immortal with a kiss.
Her lips suck forth my soul: see, where it flies!
Come, Helen, come, give me my soul again.
Here will I dwell, for heaven is in these lips,
And all is dross that is not Helena.
I will be Paris, and for love of thee,
Instead of Troy, shall Wittenberg be sack'd;
And I will combat with weak Menelaus,
And wear thy colours on my plumed crest;
Yea, I will wound Achilles in the heel,
And then return to Helen for a kiss.
O, thou art fairer than the evening air
Clad in the beauty of a thousand stars;
Brighter art thou than flaming Jupiter
When he appear'd to hapless Semele;
More lovely than the monarch of the sky
In wanton Arethusa's azur'd arms;
And none but thou shalt be my paramour!

Amoretti LXXV: One Day I Wrote her Name

Edmund Spenser

One day I wrote her name upon the strand,
But came the waves and washed it away:
Again I wrote it with a second hand,
But came the tide, and made my pains his prey.
'Vain man,' said she, 'that dost in vain assay,
A mortal thing so to immortalize;
For I myself shall like to this decay,
And eke my name be wiped out likewise.'
'Not so,' (quod I) 'let baser things devise
To die in dust, but you shall live by fame:
My verse your vertues rare shall eternize,
And in the heavens write your glorious name:
Where when as death shall all the world subdue,
Our love shall live, and later life renew.'

15

Her Lips are Copper Wire

Jean Toomer

Whisper of yellow globes
Gleaming on lamp-posts that sway
Like bootleg licker drinkers in the fog

And let your breath be moist against me
Like bright beads on yellow globes

Telephone the power-house
That the main wires are insulate

(Her words play softly up and down
dewy corridors of billboards)

Then with your tongue remove the tape
And press your lips to mine
Till they are incandescent

16

To His Coy Mistress

Andrew Marvell

Had we but world enough, and time,
This coyness, Lady, were no crime.
We would sit down and think which way
To walk and pass our long love's day.
Thou by the Indian Ganges' side
Shouldst rubies find: I by the tide
Of Humber would complain. I would
Love you ten years before the Flood,
And you should, if you please, refuse
Till the conversion of the Jews.
My vegetable love should grow
Vaster than empires, and more slow;
An hundred years should go to praise
Thine eyes and on thy forehead gaze;
Two hundred to adore each breast;
But thirty thousand to the rest;
An age at least to every part,
And the last age should show your heart;
For, Lady, you deserve this state,
Nor would I love at lower rate.
   But at my back I always hear

Time's wingèd chariot hurrying near;
And yonder all before us lie
Deserts of vast eternity.
Thy beauty shall no more be found,
Nor, in thy marble vault, shall sound
My echoing song: then worms shall try
That long preserved virginity,
And your quaint honour turn to dust,
And into ashes all my lust:
The grave's a fine and private place,
But none, I think, do there embrace.
Now therefore, while the youthful hue
Sits on thy skin like morning dew,
And while thy willing soul transpires
At every pore with instant fires,
Now let us sport us while we may,
And now, like amorous birds of prey,
Rather at once our time devour
Than languish in his slow-chapt power.
Let us roll all our strength and all
Our sweetness up into one ball,
And tear our pleasures with rough strife
Thorough the iron gates of life:
Thus, though we cannot make our sun
Stand still, yet we will make him run.

17

What Lips My Lips Have Kissed, and Where, and Why (Sonnet XLIII)

Edna St. Vincent Millay

What lips my lips have kissed, and where, and why,
I have forgotten, and what arms have lain
Under my head till morning; but the rain
Is full of ghosts tonight, that tap and sigh
Upon the glass and listen for reply,
And in my heart there stirs a quiet pain
For unremembered lads that not again
Will turn to me at midnight with a cry.
Thus in winter stands the lonely tree,
Nor knows what birds have vanished one by one,
Yet knows its boughs more silent than before:
I cannot say what loves have come and gone,
I only know that summer sang in me
A little while, that in me sings no more.

18

This is Love
A Selection from the Divani Shamsi Tabriz

Jalalu'd-din Rumi, Translated by Frederick Hadland Davis

This is Love: to fly heavenward,
To rend, every instant, a hundred veils.
The first moment, to renounce Life:
The last step, to feel without feet.
To regard this world as invisible,
Not to see what appears to one's self.
'O heart,' I said, 'may it bless thee
To have entered the circle of lovers,
To look beyond the range of the eye,
To penetrate the windings of the bosom!
Whence did this breath come to thee, O my soul,
Whence this throbbing, O my heart?'

I Shall Forget You Presently, My Dear (Sonnet IV)

Edna St. Vincent Millay

I shall forget you presently, my dear,
So make the most of this, your little day,
Your little month, your little half a year
Ere I forget, or die, or move away,
And we are done forever; by and by
I shall forget you, as I said, but now,
If you entreat me with your loveliest lie
I will protest you with my favorite vow.
I would indeed that love were longer-lived,
And vows were not so brittle as they are,
But so it is, and nature has contrived
To struggle on without a break thus far,—
Whether or not we find what we are seeking
Is idle, biologically speaking.

Never Give All the Heart

W. B. Yeats

Never give all the heart, for love
Will hardly seem worth thinking of
To passionate women if it seem
Certain, and they never dream
That it fades out from kiss to kiss;
For everything that's lovely is
But a brief, dreamy, kind delight.
O never give the heart outright,
For they, for all smooth lips can say,
Have given their hearts up to the play.
And who could play it well enough
If deaf and dumb and blind with love?
He that made this knows all the cost,
For he gave all his heart and lost.

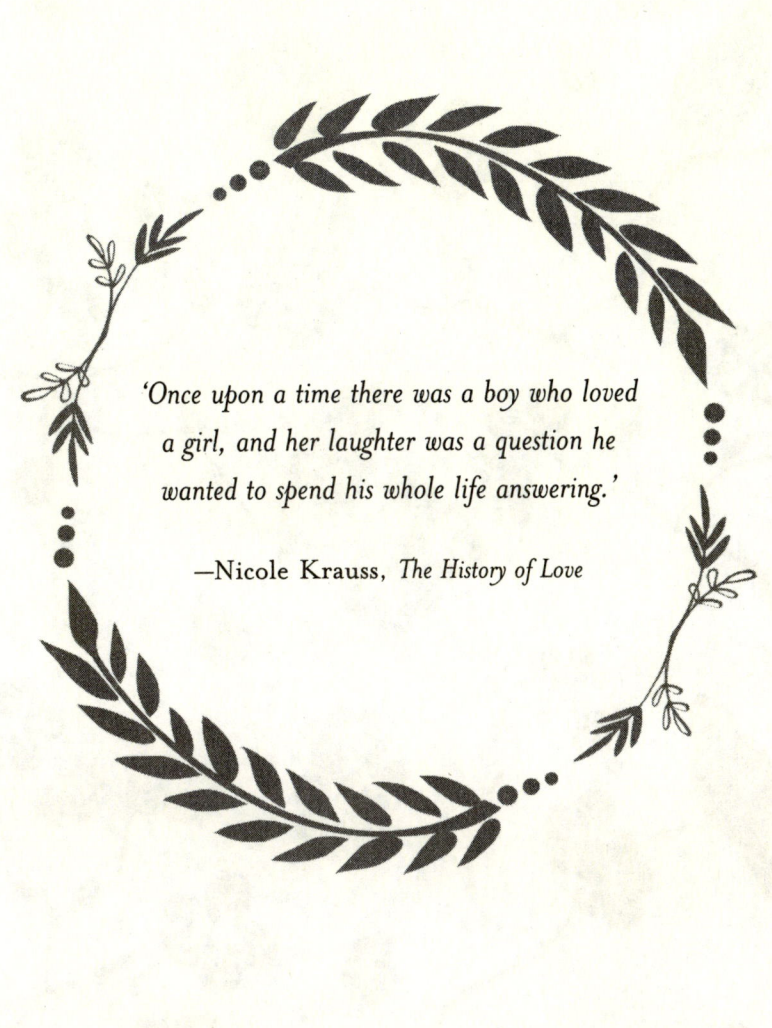

'Once upon a time there was a boy who loved a girl, and her laughter was a question he wanted to spend his whole life answering.'

—Nicole Krauss, *The History of Love*

21

I Do Not Love Thee

Caroline Elizabeth Sarah Norton

I do not love thee!—no! I do not love thee!
And yet when thou art absent I am sad;
   And envy even the bright blue sky above thee,
Whose quiet stars may see thee and be glad.

I do not love thee!—yet, I know not why,
Whate'er thou dost seems still well done, to me:
   And often in my solitude I sigh
That those I do love are not more like thee!

I do not love thee!—yet, when thou art gone,
I hate the sound (though those who speak be dear)
   Which breaks the lingering echo of the tone
Thy voice of music leaves upon my ear.

I do not love thee!—yet thy speaking eyes,
With their deep, bright, and most expressive blue,
   Between me and the midnight heaven arise,
Oftener than any eyes I ever knew.

I know I do not love thee! yet, alas!
Others will scarcely trust my candid heart;
   And oft I catch them smiling as they pass,
Because they see me gazing where thou art.

22

Love's Secret

William Blake

Never seek to tell thy love,
   Love that never told can be;
For the gentle wind doth move
   Silently, invisibly.
I told my love, I told my love,
   I told her all my heart,
Trembling, cold, in ghastly fears.
   Ah! she did depart!
Soon after she was gone from me,
   A traveller came by,
Silently, invisibly:
   He took her with a sigh.

23

Now

Robert Browning

Out of your whole life give but a moment!
All of your life that has gone before,
All to come after it,—so you ignore,
So you make perfect the present,—condense,
In a rapture of rage, for perfection's endowment,
Thought and feeling and soul and sense—
Merged in a moment which gives me at last
You around me for once, you beneath me, above me—
Me—sure that despite of time future, time past,—
This tick of our life-time's one moment you love me!
How long such suspension may linger? Ah, Sweet—
The moment eternal—just that and no more—
When ecstasy's utmost we clutch at the core
While cheeks burn, arms open, eyes shut and lips meet!

Let Me Not to the Marriage of True Minds (Sonnet 116)

William Shakespeare

Let me not to the marriage of true minds
Admit impediments. Love is not love
Which alters when it alteration finds,
Or bends with the remover to remove.O,
no! it is an ever-fixed mark,
That looks on tempests and is never shaken;
It is the star to every wandering bark,
Whose worth's unknown, although his height be taken.
Love's not Time's fool, though rosy lips and cheeks
Within his bending sickle's compass come;
Love alters not with his brief hours and weeks,
But bears it out even to the edge of doom.
   If this be error, and upon me prov'd,
   I never writ, nor no man ever lov'd.

25

To My Dear and Loving Husband

Anne Bradstreet

If ever two were one, then surely we.
If ever man were loved by wife, then thee;
If ever wife was happy in a man,
Compare with me ye women if you can.
I prize thy love more than whole mines of gold,
Or all the riches that the East doth hold.
My love is such that rivers cannot quench,
Nor ought but love from thee give recompense.
Thy love is such I can no way repay;
The heavens reward thee manifold, I pray.
Then while we live, in love let's so persever,
That when we live no more we may live ever.

26

Love

Samuel Taylor Coleridge

All thoughts, all passions, all delights,
Whatever stirs this mortal frame,
All are but ministers of Love,
   And feed his sacred flame.
Oft in my waking dreams do I
Live o'er again that happy hour,
When midway on the mount I lay,
   Beside the ruin'd tower.
The moonshine, stealing o'er the scene,
Had blended with the lights of eve;
And she was there, my hope, my joy,
   My own dear Genevieve!
She lean'd against the armèd man,
The statue of the armèd Knight;
She stood and listen'd to my lay,
   Amid the lingering light.
Few sorrows hath she of her own,
My hope! my joy! my Genevieve!
She loves me best whene'er I sing
   The songs that make her grieve.
I play'd a soft and doleful air;
I sang an old and moving story—

An old rude song, that suited well
  That ruin wild and hoary.
She listen'd with a flitting blush,
With downcast eyes and modest grace;
For well she knew I could not choose
  But gaze upon her face.
I told her of the Knight that wore
Upon his shield a burning brand;
And that for ten long years he woo'd
  The Lady of the Land.
I told her how he pined: and ah!
The deep, the low, the pleading tone
With which I sang another's love,
  Interpreted my own.
She listen'd with a flitting blush,
With downcast eyes, and modest grace;
And she forgave me, that I gazed
  Too fondly on her face!
But when I told the cruel scorn
That crazed that bold and lovely Knight,
And that he cross'd the mountain-woods,
  Nor rested day nor night;
That sometimes from the savage den,
And sometimes from the darksome shade,
And sometimes starting up at once
  In green and sunny glade—
There came and look'd him in the face
An angel beautiful and bright;
And that he knew it was a Fiend,
  This miserable Knight!

And that, unknowing what he did,
He leap'd amid a murderous band,
And saved from outrage worse than death
　The Lady of the Land;—
And how she wept and clasp'd his knees;
And how she tended him in vain—
And ever strove to expiate
　The scorn that crazed his brain;—
And that she nursed him in a cave;
And how his madness went away,
When on the yellow forest leaves
　A dying man he lay;—
His dying words—but when I reach'd
That tenderest strain of all the ditty,
My faltering voice and pausing harp
　Disturb'd her soul with pity!
All impulses of soul and sense
Had thrill'd my guileless Genevieve;
The music and the doleful tale,
　The rich and balmy eve;
And hopes, and fears that kindle hope,
An undistinguishable throng,
And gentle wishes long subdued,
　Subdued and cherish'd long!
She wept with pity and delight,
She blush'd with love and virgin-shame;
And like the murmur of a dream,
　I heard her breathe my name.
Her bosom heaved—she stepp'd aside,

As conscious of my look she stept—
Then suddenly, with timorous eye
   She fled to me and wept.
She half enclosed me with her arms,
She press'd me with a meek embrace;
And bending back her head, look'd up,
   And gazed upon my face.
'Twas partly love, and partly fear,
And partly 'twas a bashful art,
That I might rather feel, than see,
   The swelling of her heart.
I calm'd her fears, and she was calm,
And told her love with virgin pride;
And so I won my Genevieve,
   My bright and beauteous Bride.

The Good-Morrow

John Donne

I wonder by my troth, what thou and I
Did, till we loved? Were we not wean'd till then?
But suck'd on country pleasures, childishly?
Or snorted we in the Seven Sleepers' den?
'Twas so; but this, all pleasures fancies be;
If ever any beauty I did see,
Which I desired, and got, 'twas but a dream of thee.
And now good-morrow to our waking souls,
Which watch not one another out of fear;
For love all love of other sights controls,
And makes one little room an everywhere.
Let sea-discoverers to new worlds have gone;
Let maps to other, worlds on worlds have shown;
Let us possess one world; each hath one, and is one.
My face in thine eye, thine in mine appears,
And true plain hearts do in the faces rest;
Where can we find two better hemispheres
Without sharp north, without declining west?
Whatever dies, was not mix'd equally;
If our two loves be one, or thou and I
Love so alike that none can slacken, none can die.

28

Invitation to Love

Paul Laurence Dunbar

Come when the nights are bright with stars
   Or when the moon is mellow;
Come when the sun his golden bars
   Drops on the hay-field yellow.
Come in the twilight soft and gray,
Come in the night or come in the day,
Come, O love, whene'er you may,
   And you are welcome, welcome.
You are sweet, O Love, dear Love,
You are soft as the nesting dove.
Come to my heart and bring it rest
As the bird flies home to its welcome nest.
Come when my heart is full of grief
   Or when my heart is merry;
Come with the falling of the leaf
   Or with the redd'ning cherry.
Come when the year's first blossom blows,
Come when the summer gleams and glows,
Come with the winter's drifting snows,
   And you are welcome, welcome.

An Indian Love Song

Sarojini Naidu

He

Lift up the veils that darken the delicate moon
Of thy glory and grace,
Withhold not, O love, from the night
Of my longing the joy of thy luminous face,
Give me a spear of the scented keora
Guarding thy pinioned curls,
Or a silken thread from the fringes
That trouble the dream of thy glimmering pearls;
Faint grows my soul with thy tresses' perfume
And the song of thy anklets' caprice,
Revive me, I pray, with the magical nectar
that dwells in the flower of thy kiss.

She

How shall I yield to the voice of thy pleading,
How shall I grant thy prayer,
Or give thee a rose-red silken tassel,
A scented leaf from my hair?
Or fling in the flame of thy heart's desire

the veils that cover my face,
Profane the law of my father's creed for a foe
Of my father's race?
Thy kinsmen have broken our sacred altars
and slaughtered our sacred kine,
The feud of old faiths and the blood of old
battles sever thy people and mine.

He

What are the sins of my race, Beloved,
What are my people to thee?
And what are thy shrines, and kine and kindred,
What are thy gods to me?
Love recks not of feuds and bitter follies,
Of stranger, comrade or kin,
Alike in his ear sound the temple bells
And the cry of the muezzin.
For Love shall cancel the ancient wrong
And conquer the ancient rage,
Redeem with his tears the memoried sorrow
That sullied a bygone age.

30

Give All to Love

Ralph Waldo Emerson

Give all to love;
Obey thy heart;
Friends, kindred, days,
Estate, good-fame,
Plans, credit and the Muse,—
Nothing refuse.

'T is a brave master;
Let it have scope:
Follow it utterly,
Hope beyond hope:
High and more high
It dives into noon,
With wing unspent,
Untold intent:
But it is a god,
Knows its own path
And the outlets of the sky.

It was never for the mean;
It requireth courage stout.
Souls above doubt,
Valor unbending,
It will reward,—
They shall return
More than they were,
And ever ascending.

Leave all for love;
Yet, hear me, yet,
One word more thy heart behoved,
One pulse more of firm endeavor,—
Keep thee to-day,
To-morrow, forever,
Free as an Arab
Of thy beloved.

Cling with life to the maid;
But when the surprise,
First vague shadow of surmise
Flits across her bosom young,
Of a joy apart from thee,
Free be she, fancy-free;
Nor thou detain her vesture's hem,
Nor the palest rose she flung
From her summer diadem.

Though thou loved her as thyself,
As a self of purer clay,
Though her parting dims the day,
Stealing grace from all alive;
Heartily know,
When half-gods go,
The gods arrive.

'Love is so short, forgetting is so long.'

—Pablo Neruda, *Love*

Love's Marvellous Ways

Akka Mahadevi

Look at
love's marvellous
ways:

if you shoot an arrow
plant it
till no feather shows;
if you hug
a body, bones
must crunch and crumble;
weld,
the welding must vanish.

Love is then
our lord's love

Of Love: A Sonnet

Robert Herrick

How love came in I do not know,
Whether by the eye, or ear, or no;
Or whether with the soul it came
(At first) infused with the same;
Whether in part 'tis here or there,
Or, like the soul, whole everywhere,
This troubles me: but I as well
As any other this can tell:
That when from hence she does depart
The outlet then is from the heart.

Paradise Lost, Book IV, Lines 639–652

John Milton

Eve speaks to Adam
With thee conversing I forget all time;
All seasons, and their change, all please alike.
Sweet is the breath of Morn, her rising sweet,
With charm of earliest birds: pleasant the sun,
When first on this delightful land he spreads
His orient beams, on herb, tree, fruit, and flower,
Glistering with dew; fragrant the fertile earth
After soft showers; and sweet the coming on
Of grateful Evening mild; then silent Night
With this her solemn bird and this fair moon,
And these the gems of Heaven, her starry train:
But neither breath of Morn when she ascends
With charm of earliest birds; nor rising sun
On this delightful land, nor herb, fruit, flower,
Glistering with dew; nor fragrance after showers;
Nor grateful Evening mild; nor silent Night
With this her solemn bird; nor walk by moon,
Or glittering star-light without thee is sweet

A Ditty

Sir Philip Sidney

My true-love hath my heart, and I have his,
By just exchange one to the other given:
I hold his dear, and mine he cannot miss,
There never was a better bargain driven:
  My true-love hath my heart, and I have his.
His heart in me keeps him and me in one,
My heart in him his thoughts and senses guides:
He loves my heart, for once it was his own,
I cherish his because in me it bides:
  My true-love hath my heart, and I have his.

We Two, How Long We Were Fool'd

Walt Whitman

We two, how long we were fool'd,
Now transmuted, we swiftly escape as Nature escapes,
We are Nature, long have we been absent, but now we return,
We become plants, trunks, foliage, roots, bark,
We are bedded in the ground, we are rocks,
We are oaks, we grow in the openings side by side,
We browse, we are two among the wild
herds spontaneous as any,
We are two fishes swimming in the sea together,
We are what locust blossoms are, we drop scent
around lanes mornings and evenings,
We are also the coarse smut of beasts, vegetables, minerals,
We are two predatory hawks, we soar above and look down,
We are two resplendent suns, we it is who balance
ourselves orbic and stellar, we are as two comets,
We prowl fang'd and four-footed in the
woods, we spring on prey,
We are two clouds forenoons and
afternoons driving overhead,
We are seas mingling, we are two of those cheerful waves
rolling over each other and interwetting each other,
We are what the atmosphere is, transparent,

receptive, pervious, impervious,
We are snow, rain, cold, darkness, we are each
product and influence of the globe,
We have circled and circled till we have
  arrived home again, we two,
We have voided all but freedom and all but our own joy.

The Awakening

James Weldon Johnson

I dreamed that I was a rose
That grew beside a lonely way,
Close by a path none ever chose,
And there I lingered day by day.
Beneath the sunshine and the show'r
I grew and waited there apart,
Gathering perfume hour by hour,
And storing it within my heart,
    Yet, never knew,
Just why I waited there and grew.
I dreamed that you were a bee
That one day gaily flew along,
You came across the hedge to me,
And sang a soft, love-burdened song.
You brushed my petals with a kiss,
I woke to gladness with a start,
And yielded up to you in bliss
The treasured fragrance of my heart;
    And then I knew
That I had waited there for you.

Vivien's Song

Alfred, Lord Tennyson

'In Love, if Love be Love, if Love be ours,
Faith and unfaith can ne'er be equal powers:
Unfaith in aught is want of faith in all.
'It is the little rift within the lute,
That by and by will make the music mute,
And ever widening slowly silence all.
'The little rift within the lover's lute
Or little pitted speck in garnered fruit,
That rotting inward slowly moulders all.
'It is not worth the keeping: let it go:
But shall it? answer, darling, answer, no.
And trust me not at all or all in all'.

The Definition of Love

Andrew Marvell

My Love is of a birth as rare
As 'tis for object strange and high:
It was begotten by despair
Upon Impossibility.

Magnanimous Despair alone
Could show me so divine a thing,
Where feeble Hope could ne'r have flown
But vainly flapt its Tinsel Wing.

And yet I quickly might arrive
Where my extended Soul is fixt,
But Fate does Iron wedges drive,
And alwaies crowds it self betwixt.

For Fate with jealous Eye does see
Two perfect Loves; nor lets them close:
Their union would her ruine be,
And her Tyrannick pow'er depose.

And therefore her Decrees of Steel
Us as the distant Poles have plac'd,

(Though Love's whole World on us doth wheel)
Not by themselves to be embrac'd.

Unless the giddy Heaven fall,
And Earth some new Convulsion tear;
And, us to joyn, the World should all
Be cramp'd into a Planisphere.

As Lines so Loves oblique may well
Themselves in every Angle greet:
But ours so truly Parallel,
Though infinite can never meet.

Therefore the Love which us doth bind,
But Fate so enviously debarrs,
Is the Conjunction of the Mind,
And Opposition of the Stars.

Amores (I)

E. E. Cummings

your little voice
                    Over the wires came leaping
and i felt suddenly
dizzy
         With the jostling and shouting of merry flowers
wee skipping high-heeled flames
courtesied before my eyes
                              or twinkling over to my side
Looked up
with impertinently exquisite faces
floating hands were laid upon me
I was whirled and tossed into delicious dancing
up
Up
with the pale important
                          stars and the Humorous
                                                        moon

dear girl
How i was crazy how i cried when i heard
                                    over time

and tide and death
leaping
Sweetly
      your voice

Amores (II)

E.E. Cummings

in the rain-
darkness,   the sunset
being sheathed i sit and
think of you

the holy
city which is your face
your little cheeks the streets
of smiles

your eyes half-
thrush
half-angel and your drowsy
lips where float flowers of kiss

and
there is the sweet shy pirouette
your hair
and then

your dancesong
soul.   rarely-beloved

a single star is
uttered,and i

think
    of you

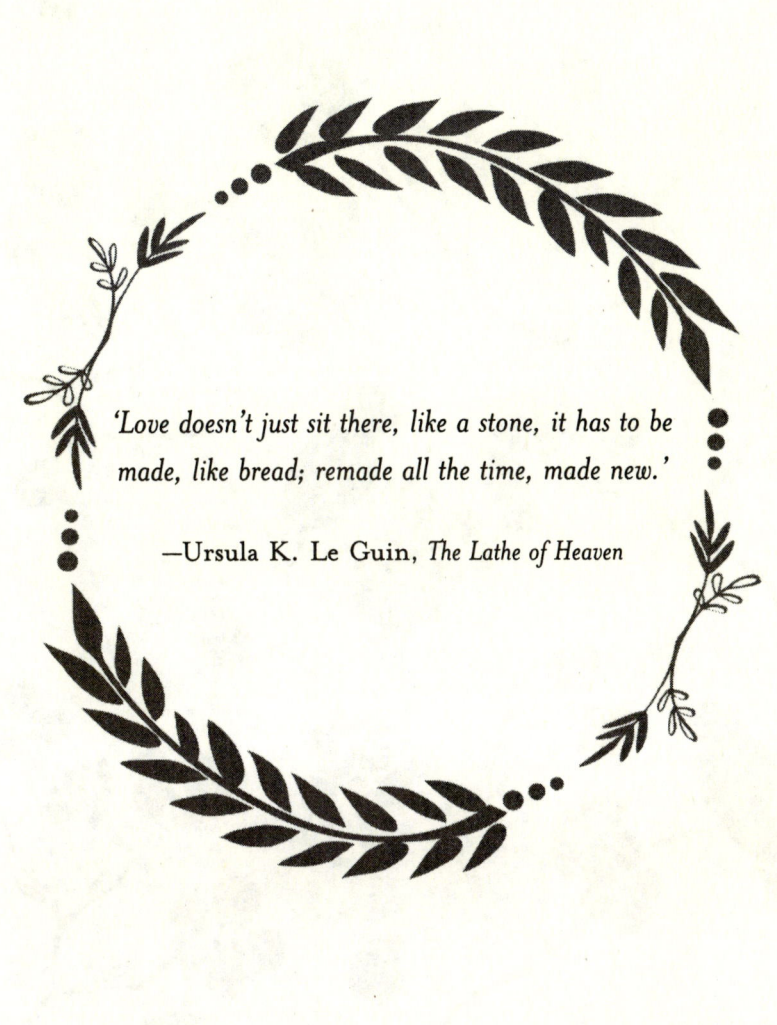

'Love doesn't just sit there, like a stone, it has to be made, like bread; remade all the time, made new.'

—Ursula K. Le Guin, *The Lathe of Heaven*

41

When You Are Old

W. B. Yeats

When you are old and grey and full of sleep,
And nodding by the fire, take down this book,
And slowly read, and dream of the soft look
Your eyes had once, and of their shadows deep;
How many loved your moments of glad grace,
And loved your beauty with love false or true,
But one man loved the pilgrim soul in you,
And loved the sorrows of your changing face;
And bending down beside the glowing bars,
Murmur, a little sadly, how Love fled
And paced upon the mountains overhead
And hid his face amid a crowd of stars.

42

The Sea of Glass

Ezra Pound

I looked and saw a sea
                    roofed over with rainbows,
In the midst of each
                    two lovers met and departed;
Then the sky was full of faces
                    with gold glories behind them.

43

Her Voice

Oscar Wilde

The wild bee reels from bough to bough
    With his furry coat and his gauzy wing.
Now in a lily-cup, and now
    Setting a jacinth bell a-swing,
        In his wandering;
Sit closer love: it was here I trow
    I made that vow,
Swore that two lives should be like one
    As long as the sea-gull loved the sea,
As long as the sunflower sought the sun,—
    It shall be, I said, for eternity
        'Twixt you and me!
Dear friend, those times are over and done.
    Love's web is spun.
Look upward where the poplar trees
    Sway in the summer air,
Here n the valley never a breeze
    Scatters the thistledown, but there
        Great winds blow fair
From the mighty murmuring mystical seas,
    And the wave-lashed leas.
Look upward where the white gull screams,

What does it see that we do not see?
Is that a star? or the lamp that gleams
    On some outward voyaging argosy,—
        Ah! can it be
We have lived our lives in a land of dreams!
        How sad it seems.
Sweet, there is nothing left to say
  But this, that love is never lost,
Keen winter stabs the breasts of May
  Whose crimson roses burst his frost,
        Ships tempest-tossed
Will find a harbor in some bay,
        And so we may.
And there is nothing left to do
  But to kiss once again, and part,
Nay, there is nothing we should rue,
  I have my beauty,—you your Art,
        Nay, do not start,
One world was not enough for two
        Like me and you.

44

All love letters Are Ridiculous

Fernando Pessoa

All love letters are
Ridiculous.
They wouldn't be love letters if they weren't
Ridiculous.

In my time I also wrote love letters
Equally, inevitably
Ridiculous.

Love letters, if there's love
Must be
Ridiculous.

But in fact
Only those who've never written
Love letters
Are
Ridiculous.

If only I could go back
To when I wrote love letters
Without thinking how
Ridiculous.

The truth is that today
My memories
Of those love letters
Are what is
Ridiculous.

(All more-than-three-syllable words,
Along with unaccountable feelings,
Are naturally
Ridiculous.)

Morning at the Window

T. S. Eliot

They are rattling breakfast plates in basement kitchens,
And along the trampled edges of the street
I am aware of the damp souls of housemaids
Sprouting despondently at area gates.
The brown waves of fog toss up to me
Twisted faces from the bottom of the street,
And tear from a passer-by with muddy skirts
An aimless smile that hovers in the air
And vanishes along the level of the roofs.

The Sun Rising

John Donne

    Busy old fool, unruly Sun,
    Why dost thou thus,
Through windows, and through curtains, call on us?
Must to thy motions lovers' seasons run?
    Saucy pedantic wretch, go chide
    Late school-boys and sour prentices,
  Go tell court-huntsmen that the king will ride,
  Call country ants to harvest offices;
Love, all alike, no season knows nor clime,
Nor hours, days, months, which are the rags of time.

    Thy beams so reverend, and strong
    Why shouldst thou think?
I could eclipse and cloud them with a wink,
But that I would not lose her sight so long．
    If her eyes have not blinded thine,
    Look, and to-morrow late tell me,
  Whether both th' Indias of spice and mine
  Be where thou left'st them, or lie here with me.
Ask for those kings whom thou saw'st yesterday,
And thou shalt hear, 'All here in one bed lay.'

    She's all states, and all princes I;
    Nothing else is;

Princes do but play us; compared to this,
All honour's mimic, all wealth alchemy.
    Thou, Sun, art half as happy as we,
      In that the world's contracted thus;
   Thine age asks ease, and since thy duties be
   To warm the world, that's done in warming us.
Shine here to us, and thou art everywhere;
This bed thy center is, these walls thy sphere.

47

Take All My Loves, My Love, Yea, Take Them All (Sonnet 40)

William Shakespeare

Take all my loves, my love, yea, take them all:
What hast thou then more than thou hadst before?
No love, my love, that thou mayst true love call;
All mine was thine before thou hadst this more.
Then if for my love thou my love receivest,
I cannot blame thee for my love thou usest;
But yet be blamed if thou this self deceivest
By wilful taste of what thyself refusest.
I do forgive thy robb'ry, gentle thief,
Although thou steal thee all my poverty;
And yet love knows it is a greater grief
To bear love's wrong than hate's known injury.
   Lascivious grace, in whom all ill well shows,
   Kill me with spites, yet we must not be foes.

Since Brass, Nor Stone, Nor Earth, Nor Boundless Sea (Sonnet 65)

William Shakespeare

Since brass, nor stone, nor earth, nor boundless sea
But sad mortality o'er-sways their power,
How with this rage shall beauty hold a plea,
Whose action is no stronger than a flower?
O, how shall summer's honey breath hold out
Against the wrackful siege of batt'ring days,
When rocks impregnable are not so stout,
Nor gates of steel so strong, but time decays?
O fearful meditation! where, alack,
Shall time's best jewel from time's chest lie hid?
Or what strong hand can hold his swift foot back?
Or who his spoil of beauty can forbid?
   O, none, unless this miracle have might,
   That in black ink my love may still shine bright.

Song: to Celia ['Drink to Me Only with Thine Eyes']

Ben Jonson

Drink to me only with thine eyes,
    And I will pledge with mine;
Or leave a kiss but in the cup,
    And I'll not look for wine.
The thirst that from the soul doth rise
    Doth ask a drink divine;
But might I of Jove's nectar sup,
    I would not change for thine.

I sent thee late a rosy wreath,
    Not so much honouring thee
As giving it a hope, that there
    It could not withered be.
But thou thereon didst only breathe,
    And sent'st it back to me;
Since when it grows, and smells, I swear,
    Not of itself, but thee.

50

I Love You

Ella Wheeler Wilcox

I love your lips when they're wet with wine
And red with a wild desire;
I love your eyes when the lovelight lies
Lit with a passionate fire.
I love your arms when the warm white flesh
Touches mine in a fond embrace;
I love your hair when the strands enmesh
Your kisses against my face.

Not for me the cold, calm kiss
Of a virgin's bloodless love;
Not for me the saint's white bliss,
Nor the heart of a spotless dove.
But give me the love that so freely gives
And laughs at the whole world's blame,
With your body so young and warm in my arms,
It sets my poor heart aflame.

So kiss me sweet with your warm wet mouth,
Still fragrant with ruby wine,
And say with a fervor born of the South
That your body and soul are mine.

Clasp me close in your warm young arms,
While the pale stars shine above,
And we'll live our whole young lives away
In the joys of a living love.

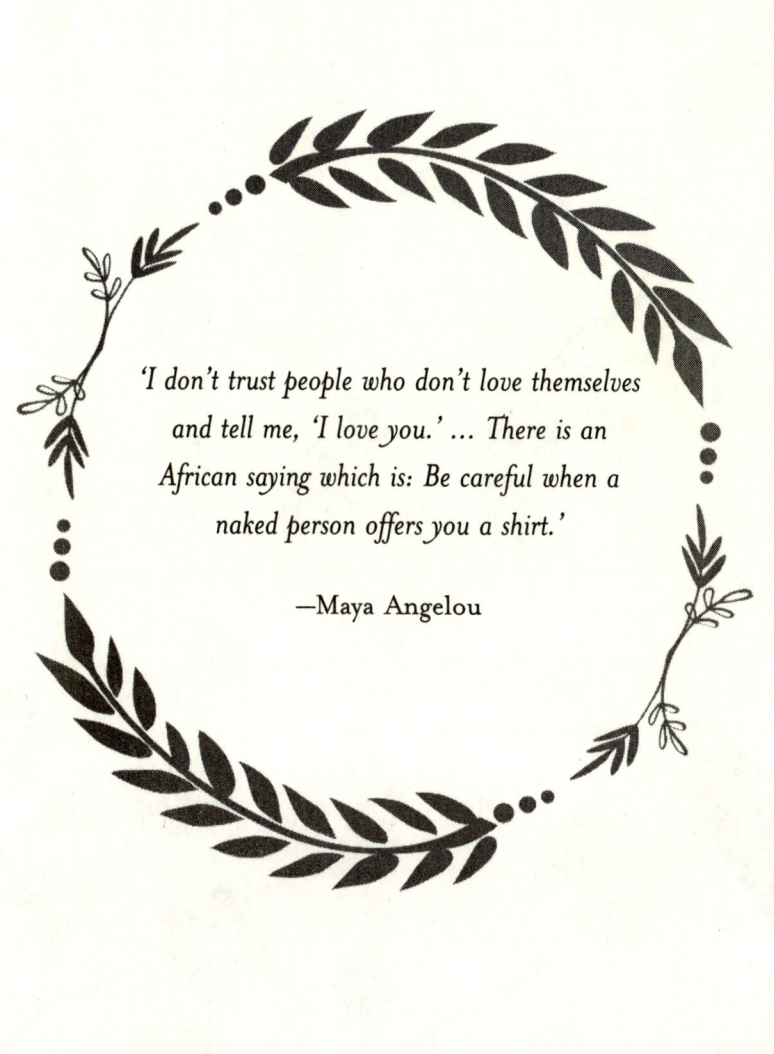

'I don't trust people who don't love themselves and tell me, 'I love you.' ... There is an African saying which is: Be careful when a naked person offers you a shirt.'

—Maya Angelou

Monna Innominata [Loved You First]

Christina Rossetti

I loved you first: but afterwards your love,
Outsoaring mine, sang such a loftier song
As drowned the friendly cooings of my dove.
Which owes the other most? My love was long,
And yours one moment seemed to wax more strong;
I loved and guessed at you, you contrued me
And loved me for what might or might not be—
Nay, weights and measures do us both a wrong.
For verily love knows not 'mine' or 'thine';
With separate 'I' and 'thou' free love has done,
For one is both and both are one in love:
Rich love knows nought of 'thine that is not mine';
Both have the strength and both the length thereof,
Both of us, of the love which makes us one.

52

Sylvia

George Etherege

The Nymph that undoes me, is fair and unkind;
No less than a wonder by Nature designed.
She's the grief of my heart, the joy of my eye;
And the cause of a flame that never can die!
Her mouth, from whence wit still obligingly flows,
Has the beautiful blush, and the smell, of the rose.
Love and Destiny both attend on her will;
She wounds with a look; with a frown, she can kill!
The desperate Lover can hope no redress;
Where Beauty and Rigour are both in excess!
In Sylvia they meet; so unhappy am I!
Who sees her, must love; and who loves her, must die!

53

Endymion

Henry Wadsworth Longfellow

The rising moon has hid the stars;
Her level rays, like golden bars,
    Lie on the landscape green,
    With shadows brown between.
And silver white the river gleams,
As if Diana, in her dreams,
    Had dropt her silver bow
    Upon the meadows low.
On such a tranquil night as this,
She woke Endymion with a kiss,
    When, sleeping in the grove,
    He dreamed not of her love.
Like Dian's kiss, unasked, unsought,
Love gives itself, but is not bought;
    Her voice, nor sound betrays
    Its deep, impassioned gaze.
It comes,—the beautiful, the free,
The crown of all humanity,—
    In silence and alone
    To seek the elected one.
It lifts the boughs, whose shadows deep,
Are Life's oblivion, the soul's sleep,

  And kisses the closed eyes
  Of him, who slumbering lies.
O, weary hearts! O, slumbering eyes!
O, drooping souls, whose destinies
  Are fraught with fear and pain,
  Ye shall be loved again!
No one is so accursed by fate,
No one so utterly desolate,
  But some heart, though unknown,
  Responds unto his own.
Responds,—as if with unseen wings,
A breath from heaven had touched its strings
  And whispers, in its song,
  'Where hast thou stayed so long!'

54

Coldness in Love

D. H. Lawrence

And you remember, in the afternoon
The sea and the sky went grey, as if there had sunk
A flocculent dust on the floor of the world: the festoon
Of the sky sagged dusty as spider cloth,
And coldness clogged the sea, till it ceased to croon.
A dank, sickening scent came up from the grime
Of weed that blackened the shore, so that I recoiled
Feeling the raw cold dun me: and all the time
You leapt about on the slippery rocks, and threw
Me words that rang with a brassy, shallow chime.
And all day long, that raw and ancient cold
Deadened me through, till the grey downs dulled to sleep.
Then I longed for you with your mantle of love to fold
Me over, and drive from out of my body the deep
Cold that had sunk to my soul, and there kept hold.
But still to me all evening long you were cold,
And I was numb with a bitter, deathly ache;
Till old days drew me back into their fold,
And dim hopes crowded me warm with companionship,
And memories clustered me close, and sleep was cajoled.
And I slept till dawn at the window blew in like dust,
Like a linty, raw-cold dust disturbed from the floor

Of the unswept sea; a grey pale light like must
That settled upon my face and hands till it seemed
To flourish there, as pale mould blooms on a crust.
And I rose in fear, needing you fearfully.
For I thought you were warm as a sudden jet of blood.
I thought I could plunge in your living hotness, and be
Clean of the cold and the must. With my hand on the latch
I heard you in your sleep speak strangely to me.
And I dared not enter, feeling suddenly dismayed.
So I went and washed my deadened flesh in the sea
And came back tingling clean, but worn and frayed
With cold, like the shell of the moon; and strange it seems
That my love can dawn in warmth again, unafraid.

Love

Rupert Brooke

Love is a breach in the walls, a broken gate,
    Where that comes in that shall not go again;
Love sells the proud heart's citadel to Fate.
    They have known shame, who love unloved. Even then,
When two mouths, thirsty each for each, find slaking,
  And agony's forgot, and hushed the crying
Of credulous hearts, in heaven—such are but taking
    Their own poor dreams within their arms, and lying
Each in his lonely night, each with a ghost.
    Some share that night. But they know love grows colder,
Grows false and dull, that was sweet lies at most.
    Astonishment is no more in hand or shoulder,
But darkens, and dies out from kiss to kiss.
All this is love; and all love is but this.

Meeting at Night

Robert Browning

The gray sea and the long black land;
And the yellow half-moon large and low:
And the startled little waves that leap
In fiery ringlets from their sleep,
As I gain the cove with pushing prow,
And quench its speed i' the slushy sand.
Then a mile of warm sea-scented beach;
Three fields to cross till a farm appears;
A tap at the pane, the quick sharp scratch
And blue spurt of a lighted match,
And a voice less loud, through joys and fears,
Than the two hearts beating each to each!

57

Take, Oh, Take Those Lips Away

John Fletcher

Take, oh, take those lips away
That so sweetly were forsworn
And those eyes, like break of day,
Lights that do mislead the morn;
But my kisses bring again,
Seals of love, though sealed in vain.

Hide, oh, hide those hills of snow,
Which thy frozen bosom bears,
On whose tops the pinks that grow
Are of those that April wears;
But first set my poor heart free,
Bound in those icy chains by thee.

Remembrance

Emily Brontë

Cold in the earth—and the deep snow piled above thee,
Far, far removed, cold in the dreary grave!
Have I forgot, my only Love, to love thee,
Severed at last by Time's all-severing wave?

Now, when alone, do my thoughts no longer hover
Over the mountains, on that northern shore,
Resting their wings where heath and fern-leaves cover
Thy noble heart forever, ever more?

Cold in the earth—and fifteen wild Decembers,
From those brown hills, have melted into spring:
Faithful, indeed, is the spirit that remembers
After such years of change and suffering!

Sweet Love of youth, forgive, if I forget thee,
While the world's tide is bearing me along;
Other desires and other hopes beset me,
Hopes which obscure, but cannot do thee wrong!

No later light has lightened up my heaven,
No second morn has ever shone for me;
All my life's bliss from thy dear life was given,
All my life's bliss is in the grave with thee.

But, when the days of golden dreams had perished,
And even Despair was powerless to destroy,
Then did I learn how existence could be cherished,
Strengthened, and fed without the aid of joy.

Then did I check the tears of useless passion—
Weaned my young soul from yearning after thine;
Sternly denied its burning wish to hasten
Down to that tomb already more than mine.

And, even yet, I dare not let it languish,
Dare not indulge in memory's rapturous pain;
Once drinking deep of that divinest anguish,
How could I seek the empty world again?

59

Wild Nights – Wild Nights!

Emily Dickinson

Wild Nights – Wild Nights!
Were I with thee
Wild Nights should be
Our luxury!
Futile – the winds –
To a heart in port –
Done with the compass –
Done with the chart!
Rowing in Eden –
Ah, the sea!
Might I moor – Tonight –
In thee!

60

The Passionate Shepherd to His Love

Christopher Marlowe

Come live with me and be my love,
And we will all the pleasures prove
That valleys, groves, hills, and fields,
Woods, or steepy mountain yields.
And we will sit upon the rocks,
Seeing the shepherds feed their flocks,
By shallow rivers to whose falls
Melodious birds sing madrigals.
And I will make thee beds of roses
And a thousand fragrant posies,
A cap of flowers, and a kirtle
Embroidered all with leaves of myrtle;
A gown made of the finest wool
Which from our pretty lambs we pull;
Fair lined slippers for the cold,
With buckles of the purest gold;
A belt of straw and ivy buds,
With coral clasps and amber studs:
And if these pleasures may thee move,
Come live with me, and be my love.

The shepherds' swains shall dance and sing
For thy delight each May morning:
If these delights thy mind may move,
Then live with me and be my love.

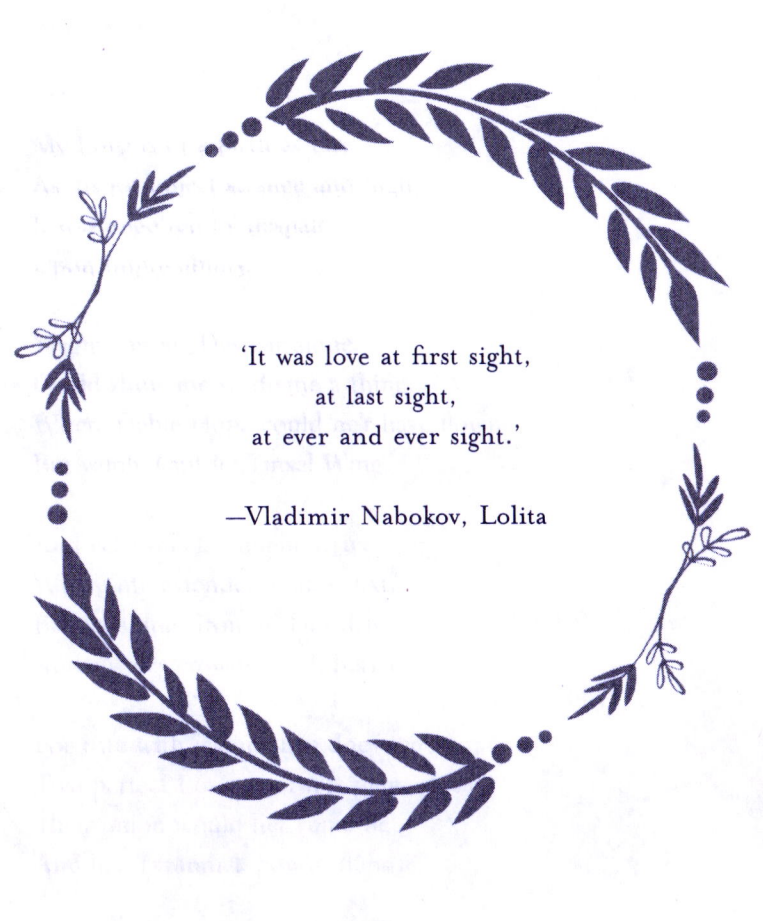

'It was love at first sight,
at last sight,
at ever and ever sight.'

—Vladimir Nabokov, Lolita

Camomile Tea

Katherine Mansfield

Outside the sky is light with stars;
There's a hollow roaring from the sea.
And, alas! for the little almond flowers,
The wind is shaking the almond tree.

How little I thought, a year ago,
In the horrible cottage upon the Lee
That he and I should be sitting so
And sipping a cup of camomile tea.

Light as feathers the witches fly,
The horn of the moon is plain to see;
By a firefly under a jonquil flower
A goblin toasts a bumble-bee.

We might be fifty, we might be five,
So snug, so compact, so wise are we!
Under the kitchen-table leg
My knee is pressing against his knee.

Our shutters are shut, the fire is low,
The tap is dripping peacefully;
The saucepan shadows on the wall
Are black and round and plain to see.

If Thou Must Love Me (Sonnet 14)

Elizabeth Barrett Browning

If thou must love me, let it be for nought
Except for love's sake only. Do not say,
'I love her for her smile—her look—her way
Of speaking gently,—for a trick of thought
That falls in well with mine, and certes brought
A sense of pleasant ease on such a day'—
For these things in themselves, Belovèd, may
Be changed, or change for thee—and love, so wrought,
May be unwrought so. Neither love me for
Thine own dear pity's wiping my cheeks dry:
A creature might forget to weep, who bore
Thy comfort long, and lose thy love thereby!
But love me for love's sake, that evermore
Thou mayst love on, through love's eternity.

63

Unending Love

Rabindranath Tagore

I seem to have loved you in numberless
forms, numberless times...
In life after life, in age after age, forever.
My spellbound heart has made and
remade the necklace of songs,
That you take as a gift, wear round your
neck in your many forms,
In life after life, in age after age, forever.

Whenever I hear old chronicles of love, its age-old pain,
Its ancient tale of being apart or together.
As I stare on and on into the past, in the end you emerge,
Clad in the light of a pole-star piercing the darkness of time:
You become an image of what is remembered forever.

You and I have floated here on the stream
that brings from the fount.
At the heart of time, love of one for another.
We have played along side millions of
lovers, shared in the same
Shy sweetness of meeting, the same
distressful tears of farewell-
Old love but in shapes that renew and renew forever.

Today it is heaped at your feet, it has found its end in you
The love of all man's days both past and forever:
Universal joy, universal sorrow, universal life.
The memories of all loves merging
with this one love of ours –
And the songs of every poet past and forever.

Love Song

Rainer Maria Rilke, Translated by Jessie Lamont

When my soul touches yours a great chord sings!
How shall I tune it then to other things?
O! That some spot in darkness could be found
That does not vibrate whene'er your depths sound.
But everything that touches you and me
Welds us as played strings sound one melody.
Where is the instrument whence the sounds flow?
And whose the master-hand that holds the bow?
O! Sweet song—

65

Sometimes with One I Love

Walt Whitman

Sometimes with one I love I fill myself with
rage for fear I effuse unreturn'd love,
But now I think there is no unreturn'd love,
the pay is certain one way or another
(I loved a certain person ardently and
my love was not return'd,
Yet out of that I have written these songs).

66

To O. E. A.

Claude McKay

Your voice is the color of a robin's breast,
    And there's a sweet sob in it like
rain—still rain in the night.
Among the leaves of the trumpet-tree, close to his nest,
    The pea-dove sings, and each note
thrills me with strange delight
Like the words, wet with music, that
well from your trembling throat.
       I'm afraid of your eyes, they're so bold,
          Searching me through, reading
my thoughts, shining like gold.
But sometimes they are gentle and soft like
the dew on the lips of the eucharis
Before the sun comes warm with his lover's kiss,
    You are sea-foam, pure with the star's loveliness,
Not mortal, a flower, a fairy, too fair
for the beauty-shorn earth,
All wonderful things, all beautiful things,
gave of their wealth to your birth:
      O I love you so much, not recking of

passion, that I feel it is wrong,
>   But men will love you, flower, fairy,
non-mortal spirit burdened with flesh,
Forever, life-long.

Evening Song

Willa Cather

Dear love, what thing of all the things that be
Is ever worth one thought from you or me,
      Save only Love,
      Save only Love?
The days so short, the nights so quick to flee,
The world so wide, so deep and dark the sea,
      So dark the sea;
So far the suns and every listless star,
Beyond their light—Ah! dear, who knows how far,
      Who knows how far?
One thing of all dim things I know is true,
The heart within me knows, and tells it you,
      And tells it you.
So blind is life, so long at last is sleep,
And none but Love to bid us laugh or weep,
      And none but Love,
      And none but Love.

Sonnet XLIV [For Thee the Sun Doth Daily Rise, and Set]

George Santayana

For thee the sun doth daily rise, and set
Behind the curtain of the hills of sleep,
And my soul, passing through the nether deep,
Broods on thy love, and never can forget.
For thee the garlands of the wood are wet,
For thee the daisies up the meadow's sweep
Stir in the sidelong light, and for thee weep
The drooping ferns above the violet.
For thee the labour of my studious ease
I ply with hope, for thee all pleasures please,
Thy sweetness doth the bread of sorrow leaven;
And from thy noble lips and heart of gold
I drink the comfort of the faiths of old,
Any thy perfection is my proof of heaven.

69

Why I Love Thee?

Sadakichi Hartmann

    Why I love thee?
  Ask why the seawind wanders,
Why the shore is aflush with the tide;
Why the moon through heaven meanders;
Like seafaring ships that ride;
On a sullen, motionless deep;
    Why the seabirds are fluttering the strand;
      Where the waves sing themselves to sleep;
        And starshine lives in the curves of the sand!

70

Oh, Oh, You Will Be Sorry for that Word!

Edna St. Vincent Millay

Oh, oh, you will be sorry for that word!
Give back my book and take my kiss instead.
Was it my enemy or my friend I heard,
'What a big book for such a little head!'
Come, I will show you now my newest hat,
And you may watch me purse my mouth and prink!
Oh, I shall love you still, and all of that.
I never again shall tell you what I think.
I shall be sweet and crafty, soft and sly;
You will not catch me reading any more:
I shall be called a wife to pattern by;
And some day when you knock and push the door,
Some sane day, not too bright and not too stormy,
I shall be gone, and you may whistle for me.

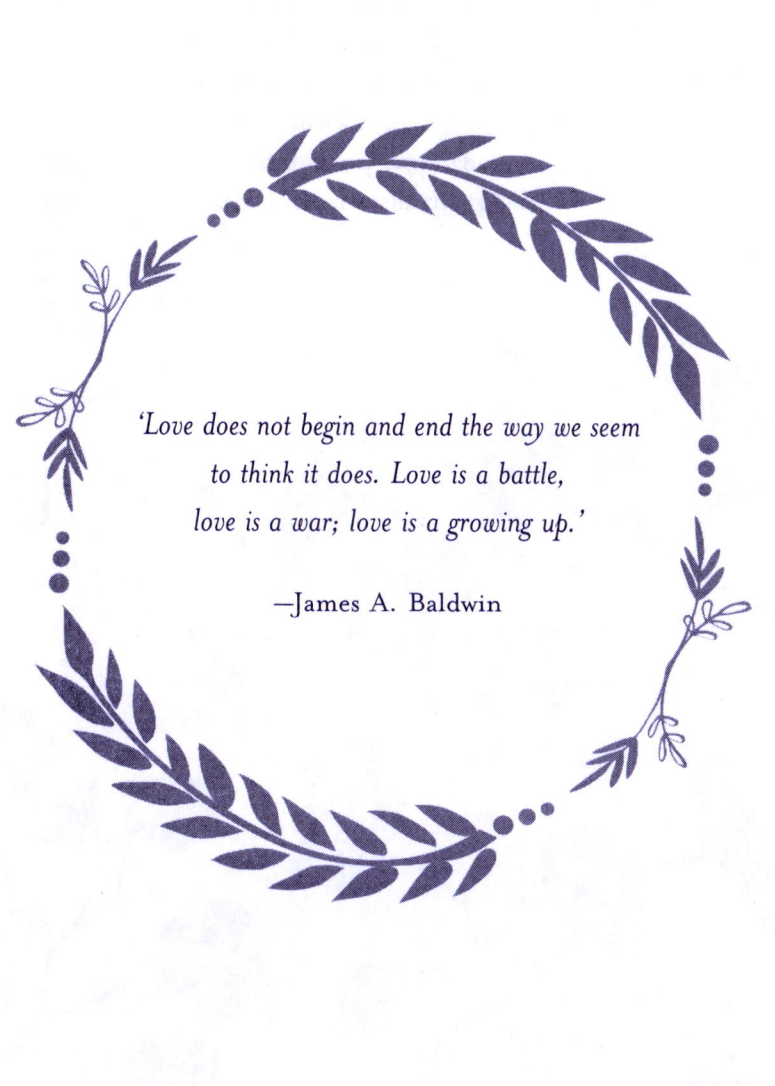

'Love does not begin and end the way we seem to think it does. Love is a battle, love is a war; love is a growing up.'

—James A. Baldwin

The Difference

Thomas Hardy

I
Sinking down by the gate I discern the thin moon,
And a blackbird tries over old airs in the pine,
But the moon is a sorry one, sad the bird's tune,
For this spot is unknown to that Heartmate of mine.

II
Did my Heartmate but haunt here at times such as now,
The song would be joyous and cheerful the moon;
But she will see never this gate, path, or bough,
Nor I find a joy in the scene or the tune.

Love and a Question

Robert Frost

A stranger came to the door at eve,
    And he spoke the bridegroom fair.
He bore a green-white stick in his hand,
    And, for all burden, care.
He asked with the eyes more than the lips
    For a shelter for the night,
And he turned and looked at the road afar
    Without a window light.
The bridegroom came forth into the porch
    With 'Let us look at the sky,
And question what of the night to be,
    Stranger, you and I.'
The woodbine leaves littered the yard,
    The woodbine berries were blue,
Autumn, yes, winter was in the wind;
    'Stranger, I wish I knew.'
Within, the bride in the dusk alone
    Bent over the open fire,
Her face rose-red with the glowing coal
    And the thought of the heart's desire.
The bridegroom looked at the weary road,
    Yet saw but her within,

And wished her heart in a case of gold
    And pinned with a silver pin.
The bridegroom thought it little to give
    A dole of bread, a purse,
A heartfelt prayer for the poor of God,
    Or for the rich a curse;
But whether or not a man was asked
    To mar the love of two
By harboring woe in the bridal house,
    The bridegroom wished he knew.

The Clod and the Pebble

William Blake

'Love seeketh not itself to please,
Nor for itself hath any care,
But for another gives its ease,
And builds a Heaven in Hell's despair.'

So sung a little Clod of Clay
Trodden with the cattle's feet,
But a Pebble of the brook
Warbled out these metres meet:

'Love seeketh only self to please,
To bind another to its delight,
Joys in another's loss of ease,
And builds a Hell in Heaven's despite.'

Because She Would Ask Me Why I Loved Her

Christopher Brennan

If questioning would make us wise
No eyes would ever gaze in eyes;
If all our tale were told in speech
No mouths would wander each to each.

Were spirits free from mortal mesh
And love not bound in hearts of flesh
No aching breasts would yearn to meet
And find their ecstasy complete.

For who is there that lives and knows
The secret powers by which he grows?
Were knowledge all, what were our need
To thrill and faint and sweetly bleed?

Then seek not, sweet, the 'If' and 'Why'
I love you now until I die.
For I must love because I live
And life in me is what you give.

75

Annabel Lee

Edgar Allen Poe

It was many and many a year ago,
    In a kingdom by the sea,
That a maiden there lived whom you may know
    By the name of Annabel Lee;
And this maiden she lived with no other thought
    Than to love and be loved by me.

I was a child and she was a child,
    In this kingdom by the sea:
But we loved with a love that was more than love—
    I and my Annabel Lee;
With a love that the winged seraphs of heaven
    Coveted her and me.

And this was the reason that, long ago,
    In this kingdom by the sea,
A wind blew out of a cloud, chilling
    My beautiful Annabel Lee;
So that her highborn kinsman came
    And bore her away from me,

To shut her up in a sepulchre
    In this kingdom by the sea.

The angels, not half so happy in heaven,
    Went envying her and me—
Yes!—that was the reason (as all men know,
    In this kingdom by the sea)
That the wind came out of the cloud by night,
    Chilling and killing my Annabel Lee.

But our love it was stronger by far than the love
    Of those who were older than we—
    Of many far wiser than we—
And neither the angels in heaven above,
    Nor the demons down under the sea,
Can ever dissever my soul from the soul
    Of the beautiful Annabel Lee.

For the moon never beams without bringing me dreams
    Of the beautiful Annabel Lee;
And the stars never rise but I feel the bright eyes
    Of the beautiful Annabel Lee;
And so, all the night-tide, I lie down by the side
Of my darling—my darling—my life and my bride,
    In the sepulchre there by the sea,
    In her tomb by the sounding sea.

To the Fair Clorinda

Aphra Behn

WHO MADE LOVE TO ME,
IMAGIN'D MORE THAN WOMAN

Fair lovely Maid, or if that Title be
Too weak, too Feminine for Nobler thee,
Permit a Name that more Approaches Truth:
And let me call thee, Lovely Charming Youth.
This last will justifie my soft complainte,
While that may serve to lessen my constraint;
And without Blushes I the Youth persue,
When so much beauteous Woman is in view
Against thy Charms we struggle but in vain
With thy deluding Form thou giv'st us pain,
While the bright Nymph betrays us to the Swain.
In pity to our Sex sure thou wer't sent,
That we might Love, and yet be Innocent:
For sure no Crime with thee we can commit;
Or if we shou'd – thy Form excuses it.
For who, that gathers fairest Flowers believes
A Snake lies hid beneath the Fragrant Leaves.

Thou beauteous Wonder of a different kind,
Soft *Cloris* with the dear *Alexis* join'd;
When e'er the Manly part of thee, wou'd plead
Thou tempts us with the Image of the Maid,
While we the noblest Passions do extend
The Love to *Hermes, Aphrodite* the Friend.

Jenny Kiss'd Me

Leigh Hunt

Jenny kiss'd me when we met,
   Jumping from the chair she sat in;
Time, you thief, who love to get
   Sweets into your list, put that in!
Say I'm weary, say I'm sad,
   Say that health and wealth have miss'd me,
Say I'm growing old, but add,
     Jenny kiss'd me.

A Winter's Tale

D. H. Lawrence

Yesterday the fields were only grey with scattered snow,
And now the longest grass-leaves hardly emerge;
Yet her deep footsteps mark the snow, and go
On towards the pines at the hills' white verge.
I cannot see her, since the mist's white scarf
Obscures the dark wood and the dull orange sky;
But she's waiting, I know, impatient and cold, half
Sobs struggling into her frosty sigh.
Why does she come so promptly, when she must know
That she's only the nearer to the inevitable farewell;
The hill is steep, on the snow my steps are slow–
Why does she come, when she knows what I have to tell?

79

The Nymph's Reply to the Shepherd

Sir Walter Raleigh

If all the world and love were young,
And truth in every Shepherd's tongue,
These pretty pleasures might me move,
To live with thee, and be thy love.

Time drives the flocks from field to fold,
When Rivers rage and Rocks grow cold,
And *Philomel* becometh dumb,
The rest complains of cares to come.

The flowers do fade, and wanton fields,
To wayward winter reckoning yields,
A honey tongue, a heart of gall,
Is fancy's spring, but sorrow's fall.

Thy gowns, thy shoes, thy beds of Roses,
Thy cap, thy kirtle, and thy posies
Soon break, soon wither, soon forgotten:
In folly ripe, in reason rotten.

Thy belt of straw and Ivy buds,
The Coral clasps and amber studs,

All these in me no means can move
To come to thee and be thy love.

But could youth last, and love still breed,
Had joys no date, nor age no need,
Then these delights my mind might move
To live with thee, and be thy love.

Air and Angels

John Donne

Twice or thrice had I loved thee,
Before I knew thy face or name;
So in a voice, so in a shapeless flame,
Angels affect us oft, and worshipped be;
   Still when, to where thou wert, I came,
Some lovely glorious nothing I did see,
   But since my soul, whose child love is,
Takes limbs of flesh, and else could nothing do,
   More subtle than the parent is
Love must not be, but take a body too,
   And therefore what thou wert, and who
     I bid love ask, and now
That it assume thy body, I allow,
And fix itself in thy lip, eye, and brow.

Whilst thus to ballast love, I thought,
And so more steadily to have gone,
With wares which would sink admiration,
I saw, I had love's pinnace overfraught,
   Every thy hair for love to work upon
Is much too much, some fitter must be sought;
   For, nor in nothing, nor in things

Extreme, and scatt'ring bright, can love inhere;
   Then as an angel, face and wings
Of air, not pure as it, yet pure doth wear,
   So thy love may be my love's sphere;
     Just such disparity
As is 'twixt air and angels' purity,
'Twixt women's love, and men's will ever be.

'I fell in love with her courage, her sincerity, and her flaming self-respect. And it's these things I'd believe in, even if the whole world indulged in wild suspicions that she wasn't all she should be. I love her and it is the beginning of everything.'

—F. Scott Fitzgerald

81

Epitaph

Lady Katherine Dyer

My dearest dust, could not thy hasty day
Afford thy drowsy patience leave to stay
One hour longer: so that we might either
Sit up, or gone to bed together?
But since thy finished labour hath possessed
Thy weary limbs with early rest,
Enjoy it sweetly; and thy widow bride
Shall soon repose her by thy slumbering side;
Whose business, now, is only to prepare
My nightly dress, and call to prayer:
Mine eyes wax heavy and the day grows old,
The dew falls thick, my blood grows cold.
Draw, draw the closed curtains: and make room:
My dear, my dearest dust; I come, I come.

From The Princess: Now Sleeps the Crimson Petal

Alfred, Lord Tennyson

Now sleeps the crimson petal, now the white;
Nor waves the cypress in the palace walk;
Nor winks the gold fin in the porphyry font.
The firefly wakens; waken thou with me.

   Now droops the milk-white peacock like a ghost,
And like a ghost she glimmers on to me.

   Now lies the Earth all Danaë to the stars,
And all thy heart lies open unto me.

   Now slides the silent meteor on, and leaves
A shining furrow, as thy thoughts in me.

   Now folds the lily all her sweetness up,
And slips into the bosom of the lake.
So fold thyself, my dearest, thou, and slip
Into my bosom and be lost in me.

83

Donal Og

Isabella Augusta, Lady Gregory

Translated from an anonymous eighth-century Irish poem

It is late last night the dog was speaking of you;
the snipe was speaking of you in her deep marsh.
It is you are the lonely bird through the woods;
and that you may be without a mate until you find me.

You promised me, and you said a lie to me,
that you would be before me where the sheep are flocked;
I gave a whistle and three hundred cries to you,
and I found nothing there but a bleating lamb.

You promised me a thing that was hard for you,
a ship of gold under a silver mast;
twelve towns with a market in all of them,
and a fine white court by the side of the sea.

You promised me a thing that is not possible,
that you would give me gloves of the skin of a fish;
that you would give me shoes of the skin of a bird;
and a suit of the dearest silk in Ireland.

When I go by myself to the Well of Loneliness,
I sit down and I go through my trouble;
when I see the world and do not see my boy,
he that has an amber shade in his hair.

It was on that Sunday I gave my love to you;
the Sunday that is last before Easter Sunday.
And myself on my knees reading the Passion;
and my two eyes giving love to you for ever.

My mother said to me not to be talking with you today,
or tomorrow, or on the Sunday;
it was a bad time she took for telling me that;
it was shutting the door after the house was robbed.

My heart is as black as the blackness of the sloe,
or as the black coal that is on the smith's forge;
or as the sole of a shoe left in white halls;
it was you that put that darkness over my life.

You have taken the east from me;
you have taken the west from me;
you have taken what is before me and what is behind me;
you have taken the moon, you have taken the sun from me;
and my fear is great that you have taken God from me!

84

Whoso List to Hunt, I Know Where Is an Hind

Thomas Wyatt

Whoso list to hunt, I know where is an hind,
But as for me, *hélas*, I may no more.
The vain travail hath wearied me so sore,
I am of them that farthest cometh behind.
Yet may I by no means my wearied mind
Draw from the deer, but as she fleeth afore
Fainting I follow. I leave off therefore,
Sithens in a net I seek to hold the wind.
Who list her hunt, I put him out of doubt,
As well as I may spend his time in vain.
And graven with diamonds in letters plain
There is written, her fair neck round about:
Noli me tangere, for Caesar's I am,
And wild for to hold, though I seem tame.

They Flee from Me

Thomas Wyatt

They flee from me, that sometime did me seek,
With naked foot stalking in my chamber.
I have seen them, gentle, tame, and meek,
That now are wild, and do not remember
That sometime they put themselves in danger
To take bread at my hand; and now they range,
Busily seeking with a continual change.

Thanked be Fortune it hath been otherwise,
Twenty times better; but once in special,
In thin array, after a pleasant guise,
When her loose gown from her shoulders did fall,
And she me caught in her arms long and small,
And therewith all sweetly did me kiss
And softly said, 'Dear heart, how like you this?'

It was no dream, I lay broad waking.
But all is turned, thorough my gentleness,
Into a strange fashion of forsaking;
And I have leave to go, of her goodness,
And she also to use newfangleness.
But since that I so kindely am served,
I fain sould know what she hath deserved.

At Last

Elizabeth Akers Allen

At last, when all the summer shine
That warmed life's early hours is past,
Your loving fingers seek for mine
And hold them close—at last—at last!
Not oft the robin comes to build
Its nest upon the leafless bough
By autumn robbed, by winter chilled,—
But you, dear heart, you love me now.
Though there are shadows on my brow
And furrows on my cheek, in truth,—
The marks where Time's remorseless plough
Broke up the blooming sward of Youth,
Though fled is every girlish grace
Might win or hold a lover's vow,
Despite my sad and faded face,
And darkened heart, you love me now!
I count no more my wasted tears;
They left no echo of their fall;
I mourn no more my lonesome years;
This blessed hour atones for all.

I fear not all that Time or Fate
May bring to burden heart or brow,—
Strong in the love that came so late,
Our souls shall keep it always now!

87

Perfect Woman

William Wordsworth

She was a phantom of delight
When first she gleam'd upon my sight;
A lovely apparition, sent
To be a moment's ornament;
Her eyes as stars of twilight fair;
Like twilight's, too, her dusky hair;
But all things else about her drawn
From May-time and the cheerful dawn;
A dancing shape, an image gay,
To haunt, to startle, and waylay.
I saw her upon nearer view,
A Spirit, yet a Woman too!
Her household motions light and free,
And steps of virgin liberty;
A countenance in which did meet
Sweet records, promises as sweet;
A creature not too bright or good
For human nature's daily food;
For transient sorrows, simple wiles,
Praise, blame, love, kisses, tears, and smiles.
And now I see with eye serene
The very pulse of the machine;

A being breathing thoughtful breath,
A traveller between life and death;
The reason firm, the temperate will,
Endurance, foresight, strength, and skill;
A perfect Woman, nobly plann'd,
To warn, to comfort, and command;
And yet a Spirit still, and bright
With something of angelic light.

88

Aedh Wishes for the Cloths of Heaven

W. B. Yeats

Had I the heavens' embroidered cloths,
Enwrought with golden and silver light,
The blue and the dim and the dark cloths
Of night and light and the half light,
I would spread the cloths under your feet:
But I, being poor, have only my dreams;
I have spread my dreams under your feet;
Tread softly because you tread on my dreams.

Love and Friendship

Emily Brontë

Love is like the wild rose-briar,
Friendship like the holly-tree—
The holly is dark when the rose-briar blooms
But which will bloom most constantly?

The wild rose-briar is sweet in spring,
Its summer blossoms scent the air;
Yet wait till winter comes again
And who will call the wild-briar fair?

Then scorn the silly rose-wreath now
And deck thee with the holly's sheen,
That when December blights thy brow
He still may leave thy garland green.

The Mortal Lease

Edith Wharton

II.

Because our kiss is as the moon to draw
The mounting waters of that red-lit sea
That circles brain with sense, and bids us be
The playthings of an elemental law,
Shall we forego the deeper touch of awe
On love's extremest pinnacle, where we,
Winging the vistas of infinity,
Gigantic on the mist our shadows saw?

Shall kinship with the dim first-moving clod
Not draw the folded pinion from the soul,
And shall we not, by spirals vision-trod,
Reach upward to some still-retreating goal,
As earth, escaping from the night's control,
Drinks at the founts of morning like a god?

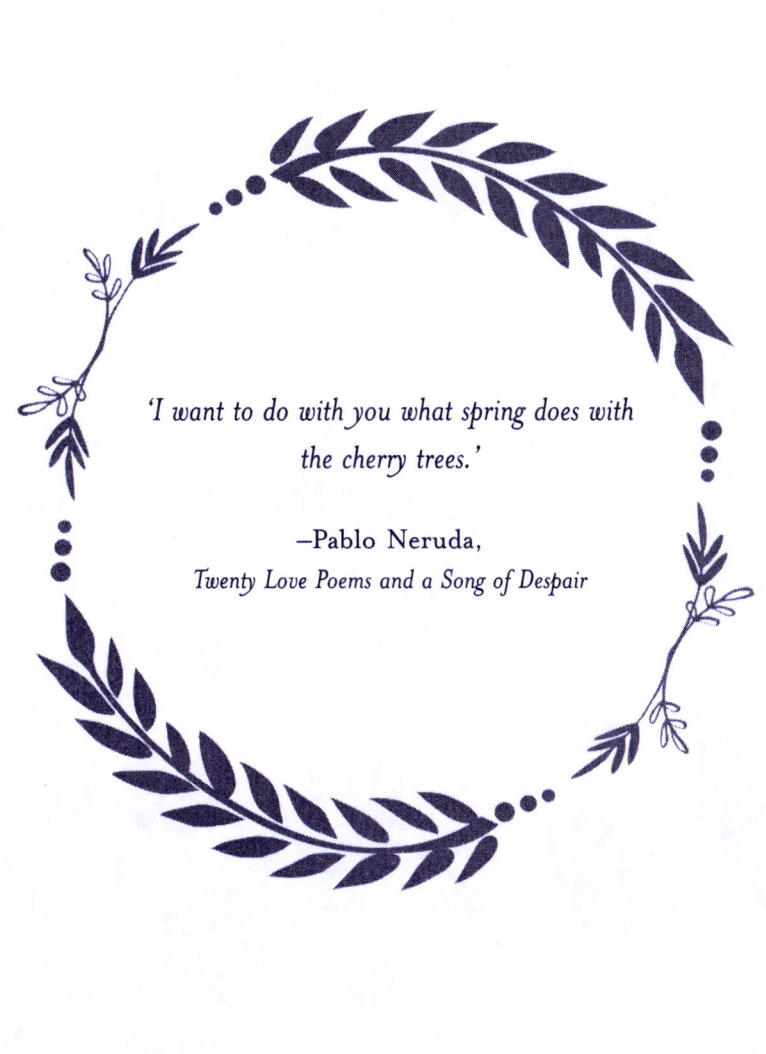

'I want to do with you what spring does with the cherry trees.'

—Pablo Neruda,
Twenty Love Poems and a Song of Despair

91

A Triad

Christina Rossetti

Three sang of love together: one with lips
   Crimson, with cheeks and bosom in a glow,
Flushed to the yellow hair and finger tips;
   And one there sang who soft and smooth as snow
   Bloomed like a tinted hyacinth at a show;
And one was blue with famine after love,
   Who like a harpstring snapped rang harsh and low
The burden of what those were singing of.
One shamed herself in love; one temperately
   Grew gross in soulless love, a sluggish wife;
One famished died for love. Thus two of three
   Took death for love and won him after strife;
One droned in sweetness like a fattened bee:
   All on the threshold, yet all short of life.

I am Mad with Love

Mirabai

I am mad with love
And no one understands my plight.
Only the wounded
Understand the agonies of the wounded,
When the fire rages in the heart.
Only the jeweller knows the value of the jewel,
Not the one who lets it go.
In pain I wander from door to door,
But could not find a doctor.
Says Mira: Harken, my Master,
Mira's pain will subside
When Shyam comes as the doctor.

Song

Paul Laurence Dunbar

My heart to thy heart,
   My hand to thine;
My lip to thy lips,
   Kisses are wine
Brewed for the lover in sunshine and shade;
Let me drink deep, then, my African maid.

Lily to lily,
   Rose unto rose;
My love to thy love
   Tenderly grows.
Rend not the oak and the ivy in twain,
Nor the swart maid from her swarthier swain.

The Sorrow of True Love

Edward Thomas

The sorrow of true love is a great sorrow
And true love parting blackens a bright morrow:
Yet almost they equal joys, since their despair
Is but hope blinded by its tears, and clear
Above the storm the heavens wait to be seen.
But greater sorrow from less love has been
That can mistake lack of despair for hope
And knows not tempest and the perfect scope
Of summer, but a frozen drizzle perpetual
Of drops that from remorse and pity fall
And cannot ever shine in the sun or thaw,
Removed eternally from the sun's law.

XXIII [Places among the Stars]

Stephen Crane

Places among the stars,
Soft gardens near the sun,
Keep your distant beauty;
Shed no beams upon my weak heart.
Since she is here
In a place of blackness,
Not your golden days
Not your silver nights
Can call me to you.
Since she is here
In a place of blackness,
Here I stay and wait.

Hid My Love

John Clare

I hid my love when young till I
Couldn't bear the buzzing of a fly;
I hid my love to my despite
Till I could not bear to look at light:
I dare not gaze upon her face
But left her memory in each place;
Where'er I saw a wild flower lie
I kissed and bade my love good-bye.
I met her in the greenest dells,
Where dewdrops pearl the wood bluebells;
The lost breeze kissed her bright blue eye,
The bee kissed and went singing by,
A sunbeam found a passage there,
A gold chain round her neck so fair;
As secret as the wild bee's song
She lay there all the summer long.
I hid my love in field and town
Till e'en the breeze would knock me down;
The bees seemed singing ballads o'er,
The fly's bass turned a lion's roar;

And even silence found a tongue,
To haunt me all the summer long;
The riddle nature could not prove
Was nothing else but secret love.

The City is Peopled

H. D.

The city is peopled
with spirits, not ghosts, O my love:
Though they crowded between
and usurped the kiss of my mouth
their breath was your gift,
their beauty, your life.

To Helen

Edgar Allan Poe

Helen, thy beauty is to me
    Like those Nicean barks of yore,
That gently, o'er a perfumed sea,
    The weary, way-worn wanderer bore
    To his own native shore.

On desperate seas long wont to roam,
    Thy hyacinth hair, thy classic face,
Thy Naiad airs have brought me home
    To the glory that was Greece.
And the grandeur that was Rome.

Lo! in yon brilliant window-niche
    How statue-like I see thee stand!
    The agate lamp within thy hand,
Ah! Psyche from the regions which
    Are Holy Land!

When I Heard at the Close of Day

Walt Whitman

When I heard at the close of the day how my name had been receiv'd with plaudits in the capitol, still it was not a happy night for me that follow'd,
And else when I carous'd, or when my plans were accomplish'd, still I was not happy,
But the day when I rose at dawn from the bed of perfect health, refresh'd, singing, inhaling the ripe breath of autumn,
When I saw the full moon in the west grow pale and disappear in the morning light,
When I wander'd alone over the beach, and undressing bathed, laughing with the cool waters, and saw the sun rise,
And when I thought how my dear friend my lover was on his way coming, O then I was happy,
O then each breath tasted sweeter, and all that day my food nourish'd me more, and the beautiful day pass'd well,
And the next came with equal joy, and with the next at evening came my friend,
And that night, while all was still I heard the waters roll slowly continually up the shores,
I heard the hissing rustle of the liquid and sands as directed to me whispering to congratulate me,

For the one I love most lay sleeping by me under the same cover in the cool night,
In the stillness in the autumn moonbeams his face was inclined toward me,
And his arm lay lightly around my breast—and that night I was happy.

The Lovers

Jalalu'd-din Rumi, Translated by Shahram Shiva

The lovers
will drink wine night and day.
They will drink until they can
tear away the veils of intellect and
melt away the layers of shame and modesty.
When in Love,
body, mind, heart and soul don't even exist.
Become this,
fall in Love, and you will not be separated again.

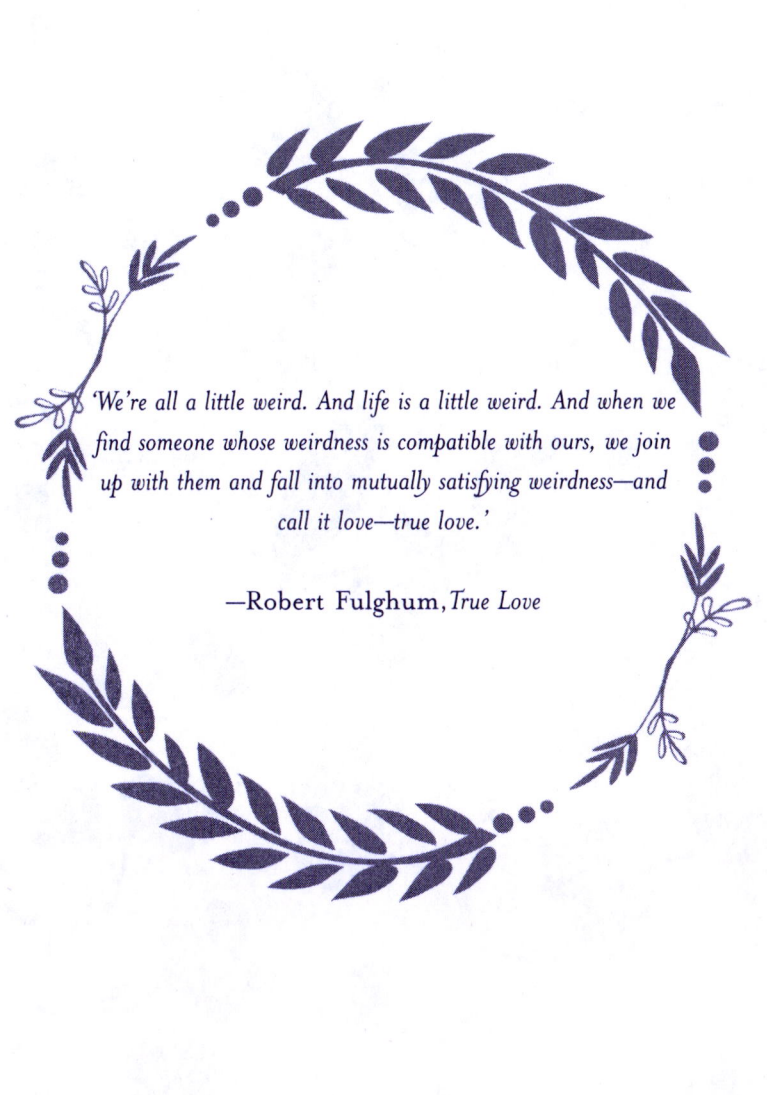

'We're all a little weird. And life is a little weird. And when we find someone whose weirdness is compatible with ours, we join up with them and fall into mutually satisfying weirdness—and call it love—true love.'

—Robert Fulghum, *True Love*